50 Flavorful Dips and Spreads for Entertaining

By: Kelly Johnson

Table of Contents

- Classic Hummus
- Guacamole
- Spinach Artichoke Dip
- Buffalo Chicken Dip
- Baba Ganoush
- Roasted Red Pepper Hummus
- Tzatziki Sauce
- Salsa Verde
- Black Bean Dip
- Queso Blanco
- Creamy Ranch Dip
- Feta Cheese Spread
- Thai Peanut Sauce
- Pimento Cheese Spread
- Avocado Feta Dip
- Caramelized Onion Dip
- Smoky Chipotle Salsa
- Cilantro Lime Yogurt Dip
- White Bean Dip with Rosemary
- Sweet Potato and Black Bean Dip
- Mediterranean Olive Tapenade
- Cilantro Mint Chutney
- Maple Bacon Dip
- Pumpkin Cream Cheese Spread
- Roasted Garlic Dip
- Easy Cheese Ball
- Dill and Cucumber Yogurt Dip
- Spicy Tuna Dip
- Cranberry Brie Bites
- Creamy Sun-Dried Tomato Dip

- Coconut Curry Dip
- Greek Yogurt Spinach Dip
- Red Curry Hummus
- Zucchini and Feta Dip
- Maple Mustard Dip
- Dill Pickle Dip
- Jalapeño Popper Dip
- Sweet and Spicy Salsa
- Avocado Lime Dip
- Garlic and Herb Cheese Spread
- Chocolate Hummus
- Bacon Cheddar Dip
- Roasted Beet Dip
- Almond Butter Dip
- Mustard Herb Dip
- Honey Walnut Cheese Spread
- Eggplant Dip (Melitzanosalata)
- Chipotle Lime Avocado Dip
- Coconut Yogurt Dip
- Apple Cider Vinegar Dressing Dip

Classic Hummus

Ingredients:

- 1 can (15 oz) chickpeas, drained and rinsed
- 1/4 cup tahini
- 1/4 cup fresh lemon juice (about 1 large lemon)
- 2 tablespoons olive oil
- 1 clove garlic, minced
- 1/2 teaspoon ground cumin
- Salt to taste
- Water, as needed
- Paprika and olive oil for garnish

Instructions:

1. **Blend Ingredients:** In a food processor, combine chickpeas, tahini, lemon juice, olive oil, garlic, cumin, and salt.
2. **Process Until Smooth:** Blend until smooth, adding water gradually to achieve desired consistency.
3. **Taste and Adjust:** Adjust seasoning as necessary.
4. **Serve:** Transfer to a serving dish, drizzle with olive oil, and sprinkle with paprika.

Guacamole

Ingredients:

- 2 ripe avocados
- 1 small onion, finely chopped
- 1 tomato, diced
- 1 lime, juiced
- 1 clove garlic, minced
- Salt and pepper to taste
- Fresh cilantro, chopped (optional)

Instructions:

1. **Mash Avocados:** In a bowl, mash the avocados with a fork until creamy but still chunky.
2. **Add Ingredients:** Stir in onion, tomato, lime juice, garlic, salt, and pepper.
3. **Mix Well:** Combine until everything is well mixed.
4. **Serve:** Garnish with cilantro if desired, and serve with tortilla chips or veggies.

Spinach Artichoke Dip

Ingredients:

- 1 cup frozen spinach, thawed and drained
- 1 can (14 oz) artichoke hearts, drained and chopped
- 1/2 cup cream cheese, softened
- 1/4 cup sour cream
- 1/4 cup mayonnaise
- 1/2 cup grated Parmesan cheese
- 1/2 cup shredded mozzarella cheese
- 1 clove garlic, minced
- Salt and pepper to taste

Instructions:

1. **Preheat Oven:** Preheat the oven to 350°F (175°C).
2. **Mix Ingredients:** In a mixing bowl, combine spinach, artichokes, cream cheese, sour cream, mayonnaise, Parmesan, mozzarella, garlic, salt, and pepper.
3. **Transfer to Baking Dish:** Pour the mixture into a baking dish and spread evenly.
4. **Bake:** Bake for 25-30 minutes, until bubbly and golden on top.
5. **Serve:** Serve warm with chips or bread.

Buffalo Chicken Dip

Ingredients:

- 2 cups shredded cooked chicken
- 1/2 cup cream cheese, softened
- 1/2 cup Frank's RedHot sauce (or your preferred hot sauce)
- 1/2 cup ranch dressing
- 1/2 cup shredded cheddar cheese
- 1/4 cup blue cheese crumbles (optional)
- Green onions for garnish (optional)

Instructions:

1. **Preheat Oven:** Preheat the oven to 350°F (175°C).
2. **Mix Ingredients:** In a mixing bowl, combine shredded chicken, cream cheese, hot sauce, ranch dressing, cheddar cheese, and blue cheese if using.
3. **Transfer to Baking Dish:** Spread the mixture evenly in a baking dish.
4. **Bake:** Bake for 20-25 minutes, until heated through and bubbly.
5. **Serve:** Garnish with green onions if desired, and serve with tortilla chips or celery sticks.

Baba Ganoush

Ingredients:

- 1 large eggplant
- 1/4 cup tahini
- 2 tablespoons lemon juice
- 2 cloves garlic, minced
- 2 tablespoons olive oil
- Salt to taste
- Paprika for garnish
- Fresh parsley for garnish (optional)

Instructions:

1. **Roast Eggplant:** Preheat the oven to 400°F (200°C). Prick the eggplant with a fork and place it on a baking sheet. Roast for 30-40 minutes until soft. Allow to cool, then scoop out the flesh.
2. **Blend Ingredients:** In a food processor, combine eggplant flesh, tahini, lemon juice, garlic, olive oil, and salt.
3. **Process Until Smooth:** Blend until creamy and smooth.
4. **Serve:** Transfer to a serving dish, drizzle with olive oil, and sprinkle with paprika and parsley.

Roasted Red Pepper Hummus

Ingredients:

- 1 can (15 oz) chickpeas, drained and rinsed
- 1/4 cup tahini
- 1/4 cup fresh lemon juice
- 1/2 cup roasted red peppers, chopped
- 2 tablespoons olive oil
- 1 clove garlic, minced
- Salt to taste
- Water, as needed

Instructions:

1. **Blend Ingredients:** In a food processor, combine chickpeas, tahini, lemon juice, roasted red peppers, olive oil, garlic, and salt.
2. **Process Until Smooth:** Blend until smooth, adding water gradually for desired consistency.
3. **Taste and Adjust:** Adjust seasoning as needed.
4. **Serve:** Transfer to a serving dish and drizzle with olive oil before serving.

Tzatziki Sauce

Ingredients:

- 1 cup Greek yogurt
- 1/2 cucumber, grated and drained
- 2 cloves garlic, minced
- 1 tablespoon olive oil
- 1 tablespoon fresh lemon juice
- 1 tablespoon fresh dill, chopped
- Salt and pepper to taste

Instructions:

1. **Combine Ingredients:** In a bowl, mix together Greek yogurt, grated cucumber, garlic, olive oil, lemon juice, dill, salt, and pepper.
2. **Mix Well:** Stir until all ingredients are well combined.
3. **Chill:** Refrigerate for at least 30 minutes to allow flavors to meld.
4. **Serve:** Serve as a dip or condiment with pita bread or vegetables.

Salsa Verde

Ingredients:

- 1 lb tomatillos, husked and rinsed
- 1 jalapeño, stemmed (and seeded for less heat)
- 1/2 cup onion, chopped
- 2 cloves garlic, minced
- 1/2 cup fresh cilantro, chopped
- 1 tablespoon lime juice
- Salt to taste

Instructions:

1. **Roast Tomatillos and Jalapeño:** Preheat the oven to 400°F (200°C). Place tomatillos and jalapeño on a baking sheet and roast for 15-20 minutes until slightly charred.
2. **Blend Ingredients:** In a blender, combine roasted tomatillos, jalapeño, onion, garlic, cilantro, lime juice, and salt.
3. **Blend Until Smooth:** Blend until smooth, adjusting seasoning to taste.
4. **Serve:** Serve as a dip with tortilla chips or as a sauce for tacos and grilled meats.

Enjoy these delicious dips and spreads at your next gathering!

Black Bean Dip

Ingredients:

- 1 can (15 oz) black beans, drained and rinsed
- 1 clove garlic, minced
- 1/2 teaspoon ground cumin
- 1/2 teaspoon chili powder
- 1 tablespoon lime juice
- Salt and pepper to taste
- 1 tablespoon olive oil
- Fresh cilantro for garnish (optional)

Instructions:

1. **Blend Ingredients:** In a food processor, combine black beans, garlic, cumin, chili powder, lime juice, salt, pepper, and olive oil.
2. **Process Until Smooth:** Blend until creamy and smooth, adding a splash of water if needed for consistency.
3. **Taste and Adjust:** Adjust seasoning as necessary.
4. **Serve:** Transfer to a serving dish and garnish with fresh cilantro if desired.

Queso Blanco

Ingredients:

- 1 lb white American cheese, cubed
- 1 cup milk
- 1/2 cup diced tomatoes with green chilies (like Ro-Tel)
- 1/4 cup chopped onion
- 1/4 cup diced jalapeños (optional)
- Salt to taste

Instructions:

1. **Melt Cheese:** In a saucepan over medium heat, combine cheese and milk. Stir frequently until melted and smooth.
2. **Add Other Ingredients:** Stir in diced tomatoes, onion, jalapeños, and salt.
3. **Cook:** Cook for an additional 5 minutes, stirring often.
4. **Serve:** Serve warm with tortilla chips.

Creamy Ranch Dip

Ingredients:

- 1 cup sour cream
- 1/2 cup mayonnaise
- 1 tablespoon dried dill
- 1 tablespoon dried parsley
- 1 teaspoon garlic powder
- 1 teaspoon onion powder
- Salt and pepper to taste

Instructions:

1. **Combine Ingredients:** In a mixing bowl, combine sour cream, mayonnaise, dill, parsley, garlic powder, onion powder, salt, and pepper.
2. **Mix Well:** Stir until well combined.
3. **Chill:** Refrigerate for at least 30 minutes to allow flavors to meld.
4. **Serve:** Serve with fresh veggies or chips.

Feta Cheese Spread

Ingredients:

- 8 oz feta cheese, crumbled
- 1/2 cup cream cheese, softened
- 2 tablespoons olive oil
- 1 tablespoon lemon juice
- 1 clove garlic, minced
- Fresh herbs (like parsley or dill), chopped

Instructions:

1. **Blend Ingredients:** In a food processor, combine feta cheese, cream cheese, olive oil, lemon juice, garlic, and fresh herbs.
2. **Process Until Smooth:** Blend until creamy and well mixed.
3. **Taste and Adjust:** Adjust seasoning as needed.
4. **Serve:** Transfer to a serving dish and serve with pita chips or bread.

Thai Peanut Sauce

Ingredients:

- 1/2 cup peanut butter
- 1/4 cup soy sauce
- 2 tablespoons lime juice
- 2 tablespoons honey or maple syrup
- 1 clove garlic, minced
- 1 teaspoon grated fresh ginger (optional)
- Water to thin

Instructions:

1. **Combine Ingredients:** In a bowl, whisk together peanut butter, soy sauce, lime juice, honey, garlic, and ginger.
2. **Adjust Consistency:** Gradually add water until you reach desired consistency (smooth and pourable).
3. **Taste and Adjust:** Adjust seasoning to taste.
4. **Serve:** Serve with fresh vegetables, spring rolls, or as a salad dressing.

Pimento Cheese Spread

Ingredients:

- 8 oz cream cheese, softened
- 1 cup shredded sharp cheddar cheese
- 1/2 cup diced pimentos (drained)
- 1 tablespoon mayonnaise
- 1 teaspoon garlic powder
- Salt and pepper to taste

Instructions:

1. **Mix Ingredients:** In a mixing bowl, combine cream cheese, cheddar cheese, pimentos, mayonnaise, garlic powder, salt, and pepper.
2. **Stir Until Smooth:** Mix until well combined and creamy.
3. **Chill:** Refrigerate for at least 30 minutes before serving.
4. **Serve:** Serve with crackers or as a sandwich spread.

Avocado Feta Dip

Ingredients:

- 1 ripe avocado
- 4 oz feta cheese, crumbled
- 1 tablespoon lemon juice
- 2 tablespoons olive oil
- Salt and pepper to taste
- Fresh herbs (like parsley or basil), chopped

Instructions:

1. **Mash Avocado:** In a bowl, mash the avocado until smooth.
2. **Combine Ingredients:** Add feta, lemon juice, olive oil, salt, pepper, and herbs.
3. **Mix Well:** Stir until well combined.
4. **Serve:** Serve with pita chips or fresh vegetables.

Caramelized Onion Dip

Ingredients:

- 2 large onions, sliced
- 2 tablespoons olive oil
- 1 cup sour cream
- 1/2 cup cream cheese, softened
- 1/2 teaspoon garlic powder
- Salt and pepper to taste

Instructions:

1. **Caramelize Onions:** In a skillet, heat olive oil over medium heat. Add sliced onions and cook, stirring frequently, for 20-25 minutes until soft and caramelized.
2. **Cool Onions:** Remove from heat and let cool slightly.
3. **Mix Ingredients:** In a bowl, combine sour cream, cream cheese, garlic powder, salt, pepper, and cooled onions.
4. **Serve:** Serve with chips, crackers, or fresh vegetables.

Enjoy these delicious dips and spreads at your next gathering or snack time!

Smoky Chipotle Salsa

Ingredients:

- 4 medium tomatoes, roasted
- 1-2 chipotle peppers in adobo sauce (to taste)
- 1/2 onion, chopped
- 2 cloves garlic, minced
- 1 tablespoon lime juice
- Salt and pepper to taste
- Fresh cilantro for garnish (optional)

Instructions:

1. **Blend Ingredients:** In a food processor, combine roasted tomatoes, chipotle peppers, onion, garlic, lime juice, salt, and pepper.
2. **Process Until Smooth:** Blend until desired consistency is reached (smooth or chunky).
3. **Taste and Adjust:** Adjust seasoning to taste.
4. **Serve:** Transfer to a serving dish and garnish with cilantro if desired.

Cilantro Lime Yogurt Dip

Ingredients:

- 1 cup plain Greek yogurt
- 1/4 cup fresh cilantro, chopped
- 1 tablespoon lime juice
- 1 clove garlic, minced
- Salt and pepper to taste

Instructions:

1. **Combine Ingredients:** In a bowl, mix together Greek yogurt, cilantro, lime juice, garlic, salt, and pepper.
2. **Mix Well:** Stir until well combined and smooth.
3. **Chill:** Refrigerate for at least 30 minutes before serving.
4. **Serve:** Serve with fresh vegetables, chips, or as a topping for tacos.

White Bean Dip with Rosemary

Ingredients:

- 1 can (15 oz) white beans (cannellini or great northern), drained and rinsed
- 2 tablespoons olive oil
- 1 tablespoon fresh rosemary, chopped (or 1 teaspoon dried rosemary)
- 1 tablespoon lemon juice
- Salt and pepper to taste
- Optional: crushed red pepper flakes for heat

Instructions:

1. **Blend Ingredients:** In a food processor, combine white beans, olive oil, rosemary, lemon juice, salt, and pepper.
2. **Process Until Smooth:** Blend until creamy, adding a little water if needed for consistency.
3. **Taste and Adjust:** Adjust seasoning and add crushed red pepper flakes if desired.
4. **Serve:** Transfer to a serving dish and serve with pita chips or fresh veggies.

Sweet Potato and Black Bean Dip

Ingredients:

- 1 medium sweet potato, peeled and cubed
- 1 can (15 oz) black beans, drained and rinsed
- 1 teaspoon cumin
- 1 teaspoon chili powder
- 1 tablespoon lime juice
- Salt and pepper to taste
- Optional: fresh cilantro for garnish

Instructions:

1. **Cook Sweet Potato:** Boil sweet potato cubes in salted water until tender, about 15-20 minutes. Drain and cool.
2. **Blend Ingredients:** In a food processor, combine cooked sweet potato, black beans, cumin, chili powder, lime juice, salt, and pepper.
3. **Process Until Smooth:** Blend until creamy and smooth.
4. **Serve:** Transfer to a serving dish and garnish with fresh cilantro if desired.

Mediterranean Olive Tapenade

Ingredients:

- 1 cup mixed olives (green and black), pitted
- 2 tablespoons capers, drained
- 2 cloves garlic, minced
- 2 tablespoons olive oil
- 1 tablespoon lemon juice
- Fresh parsley for garnish (optional)

Instructions:

1. **Blend Ingredients:** In a food processor, combine olives, capers, garlic, olive oil, and lemon juice.
2. **Process Until Chunky:** Blend until you reach a chunky paste.
3. **Taste and Adjust:** Adjust seasoning if necessary.
4. **Serve:** Transfer to a serving dish and garnish with fresh parsley if desired. Serve with crusty bread or crackers.

Cilantro Mint Chutney

Ingredients:

- 1 cup fresh cilantro leaves
- 1/2 cup fresh mint leaves
- 1-2 green chilies (adjust to taste)
- 1 tablespoon lemon juice
- 1 teaspoon sugar (optional)
- Salt to taste
- Water as needed

Instructions:

1. **Blend Ingredients:** In a food processor, combine cilantro, mint, green chilies, lemon juice, sugar, and salt.
2. **Add Water:** Blend until smooth, adding water as needed to achieve desired consistency.
3. **Taste and Adjust:** Adjust seasoning to taste.
4. **Serve:** Serve as a dip with snacks or as a condiment with Indian dishes.

Maple Bacon Dip

Ingredients:

- 8 oz cream cheese, softened
- 1/2 cup cooked bacon, chopped
- 1/4 cup maple syrup
- 1/2 cup shredded cheddar cheese
- 1/4 cup green onions, sliced

Instructions:

1. **Combine Ingredients:** In a mixing bowl, combine cream cheese, bacon, maple syrup, cheddar cheese, and green onions.
2. **Mix Until Smooth:** Stir until well combined and creamy.
3. **Chill:** Refrigerate for at least 30 minutes before serving.
4. **Serve:** Serve with crackers or vegetables.

Pumpkin Cream Cheese Spread

Ingredients:

- 8 oz cream cheese, softened
- 1/2 cup pumpkin puree
- 1/4 cup powdered sugar
- 1 teaspoon pumpkin pie spice
- 1 teaspoon vanilla extract

Instructions:

1. **Mix Ingredients:** In a mixing bowl, combine cream cheese, pumpkin puree, powdered sugar, pumpkin pie spice, and vanilla.
2. **Mix Until Smooth:** Beat until creamy and well combined.
3. **Chill:** Refrigerate for at least 1 hour before serving.
4. **Serve:** Serve with bagels, toast, or crackers.

Enjoy these delicious dips and spreads at your next gathering or as part of your everyday snacks!

Roasted Garlic Dip

Ingredients:

- 1 head garlic
- 1 cup cream cheese, softened
- 1/2 cup sour cream
- 1 tablespoon lemon juice
- Salt and pepper to taste
- Fresh herbs for garnish (optional)

Instructions:

1. **Roast Garlic:** Preheat the oven to 400°F (200°C). Cut the top off the garlic head and drizzle with olive oil. Wrap in foil and roast for 30-35 minutes until soft.
2. **Prepare Dip:** In a bowl, squeeze out the roasted garlic cloves and mash them with a fork.
3. **Combine Ingredients:** Add cream cheese, sour cream, lemon juice, salt, and pepper. Mix until smooth and creamy.
4. **Serve:** Transfer to a serving dish, garnish with herbs if desired, and serve with crackers or veggies.

Easy Cheese Ball

Ingredients:

- 8 oz cream cheese, softened
- 1 cup shredded cheddar cheese
- 1/4 cup chopped green onions
- 1/4 cup diced bell pepper
- 1/2 teaspoon garlic powder
- 1/2 teaspoon onion powder
- Chopped nuts or herbs for rolling (optional)

Instructions:

1. **Mix Ingredients:** In a mixing bowl, combine cream cheese, cheddar cheese, green onions, bell pepper, garlic powder, and onion powder.
2. **Shape Cheese Ball:** Mix until well combined, then shape into a ball.
3. **Chill:** Wrap in plastic wrap and refrigerate for at least 1 hour.
4. **Roll and Serve:** Optional: Roll in chopped nuts or herbs before serving. Serve with crackers or bread.

Dill and Cucumber Yogurt Dip

Ingredients:

- 1 cup plain Greek yogurt
- 1/2 cup cucumber, grated and drained
- 1 tablespoon fresh dill, chopped
- 1 tablespoon lemon juice
- 1 clove garlic, minced
- Salt and pepper to taste

Instructions:

1. **Combine Ingredients:** In a bowl, mix together Greek yogurt, cucumber, dill, lemon juice, garlic, salt, and pepper.
2. **Mix Well:** Stir until well combined and smooth.
3. **Chill:** Refrigerate for at least 30 minutes to let flavors meld.
4. **Serve:** Serve with fresh veggies, pita chips, or as a sauce for grilled meats.

Spicy Tuna Dip

Ingredients:

- 1 can (5 oz) tuna, drained
- 1/4 cup mayonnaise
- 1 tablespoon sriracha (or to taste)
- 1 teaspoon soy sauce
- 1 green onion, sliced
- Salt and pepper to taste

Instructions:

1. **Mix Ingredients:** In a bowl, combine tuna, mayonnaise, sriracha, soy sauce, green onion, salt, and pepper.
2. **Mix Until Combined:** Stir until well combined and creamy.
3. **Taste and Adjust:** Adjust seasoning and spice level to taste.
4. **Serve:** Serve with crackers or tortilla chips.

Cranberry Brie Bites

Ingredients:

- 1 sheet puff pastry, thawed
- 1 small wheel of brie cheese
- 1/2 cup cranberry sauce (store-bought or homemade)
- Fresh rosemary for garnish (optional)

Instructions:

1. **Preheat Oven:** Preheat the oven to 400°F (200°C).
2. **Prepare Puff Pastry:** Roll out puff pastry and cut into squares (about 3x3 inches).
3. **Assemble Bites:** Place a square on a baking sheet. Cut brie into small pieces and place on the pastry, top with a spoonful of cranberry sauce.
4. **Bake:** Bake for 15-20 minutes until golden brown.
5. **Serve:** Garnish with fresh rosemary if desired and serve warm.

Creamy Sun-Dried Tomato Dip

Ingredients:

- 1 cup cream cheese, softened
- 1/2 cup sour cream
- 1/2 cup sun-dried tomatoes, chopped
- 1/4 cup grated Parmesan cheese
- 1 tablespoon fresh basil, chopped
- Salt and pepper to taste

Instructions:

1. **Combine Ingredients:** In a bowl, mix together cream cheese, sour cream, sun-dried tomatoes, Parmesan cheese, basil, salt, and pepper.
2. **Mix Until Smooth:** Stir until well combined and creamy.
3. **Chill:** Refrigerate for at least 30 minutes before serving.
4. **Serve:** Serve with crackers, bread, or fresh veggies.

Coconut Curry Dip

Ingredients:

- 1 cup Greek yogurt
- 1/2 cup coconut milk
- 1 tablespoon curry powder
- 1 tablespoon lime juice
- Salt to taste
- Chopped cilantro for garnish (optional)

Instructions:

1. **Combine Ingredients:** In a bowl, mix Greek yogurt, coconut milk, curry powder, lime juice, and salt.
2. **Mix Well:** Stir until smooth and well combined.
3. **Chill:** Refrigerate for at least 30 minutes to allow flavors to meld.
4. **Serve:** Serve with fresh veggies or pita chips, garnished with cilantro if desired.

Greek Yogurt Spinach Dip

Ingredients:

- 1 cup plain Greek yogurt
- 1 cup fresh spinach, chopped
- 1/4 cup mayonnaise
- 1 clove garlic, minced
- 1/2 teaspoon onion powder
- Salt and pepper to taste

Instructions:

1. **Combine Ingredients:** In a bowl, mix Greek yogurt, spinach, mayonnaise, garlic, onion powder, salt, and pepper.
2. **Mix Well:** Stir until well combined.
3. **Chill:** Refrigerate for at least 30 minutes before serving.
4. **Serve:** Serve with crackers, chips, or fresh vegetables.

Enjoy these delicious dips and appetizers at your next gathering or as a tasty snack!

Red Curry Hummus

Ingredients:

- 1 can (15 oz) chickpeas, drained and rinsed
- 1/4 cup tahini
- 2 tablespoons red curry paste
- 2 tablespoons lime juice
- 2 tablespoons olive oil
- 1-2 tablespoons water (as needed for consistency)
- Salt to taste
- Fresh cilantro for garnish (optional)

Instructions:

1. **Blend Ingredients:** In a food processor, combine chickpeas, tahini, red curry paste, lime juice, olive oil, and salt.
2. **Process Until Smooth:** Blend until smooth, adding water as needed to reach desired consistency.
3. **Taste and Adjust:** Adjust seasoning and spice level to taste.
4. **Serve:** Transfer to a bowl, garnish with cilantro if desired, and serve with pita chips or fresh vegetables.

Zucchini and Feta Dip

Ingredients:

- 2 medium zucchinis, grated
- 1 cup feta cheese, crumbled
- 1/2 cup Greek yogurt
- 1 tablespoon lemon juice
- 1 clove garlic, minced
- 1 tablespoon fresh dill, chopped (or 1 teaspoon dried dill)
- Salt and pepper to taste

Instructions:

1. **Prepare Zucchini:** In a skillet over medium heat, sauté grated zucchini until just tender (about 3-4 minutes). Drain excess moisture and let cool.
2. **Combine Ingredients:** In a bowl, mix together cooled zucchini, feta, Greek yogurt, lemon juice, garlic, dill, salt, and pepper.
3. **Mix Well:** Stir until well combined and creamy.
4. **Chill and Serve:** Refrigerate for at least 30 minutes before serving. Serve with pita bread or crackers.

Maple Mustard Dip

Ingredients:

- 1/2 cup Dijon mustard
- 1/4 cup maple syrup
- 1/4 cup mayonnaise
- 1 tablespoon apple cider vinegar
- Salt and pepper to taste

Instructions:

1. **Combine Ingredients:** In a bowl, mix together Dijon mustard, maple syrup, mayonnaise, and apple cider vinegar.
2. **Whisk Until Smooth:** Stir until smooth and well combined.
3. **Taste and Adjust:** Season with salt and pepper to taste.
4. **Serve:** Serve as a dip for pretzels, veggies, or as a sandwich spread.

Dill Pickle Dip

Ingredients:

- 8 oz cream cheese, softened
- 1/2 cup sour cream
- 1/2 cup dill pickles, chopped
- 1 tablespoon pickle juice
- 1 teaspoon dried dill
- Salt and pepper to taste

Instructions:

1. **Combine Ingredients:** In a mixing bowl, combine cream cheese, sour cream, chopped dill pickles, pickle juice, and dried dill.
2. **Mix Until Smooth:** Stir until well combined and creamy.
3. **Taste and Adjust:** Season with salt and pepper to taste.
4. **Chill and Serve:** Refrigerate for at least 30 minutes before serving. Serve with crackers or veggies.

Jalapeño Popper Dip

Ingredients:

- 8 oz cream cheese, softened
- 1 cup shredded cheddar cheese
- 1/2 cup mayonnaise
- 1/2 cup diced jalapeños (fresh or pickled)
- 1/4 teaspoon garlic powder
- 1/4 teaspoon onion powder
- Salt and pepper to taste

Instructions:

1. **Preheat Oven:** Preheat the oven to 350°F (175°C).
2. **Mix Ingredients:** In a bowl, combine cream cheese, cheddar cheese, mayonnaise, jalapeños, garlic powder, onion powder, salt, and pepper.
3. **Transfer to Baking Dish:** Spread the mixture into a baking dish.
4. **Bake:** Bake for 20-25 minutes until bubbly and golden on top.
5. **Serve:** Serve warm with tortilla chips or sliced vegetables.

Sweet and Spicy Salsa

Ingredients:

- 2 cups diced tomatoes
- 1/2 cup diced red onion
- 1/4 cup chopped fresh cilantro
- 1 jalapeño, seeded and diced
- 1 tablespoon lime juice
- 1 tablespoon honey (or to taste)
- Salt to taste

Instructions:

1. **Combine Ingredients:** In a mixing bowl, combine diced tomatoes, red onion, cilantro, jalapeño, lime juice, honey, and salt.
2. **Mix Well:** Stir until well combined.
3. **Taste and Adjust:** Adjust sweetness and seasoning to taste.
4. **Chill and Serve:** Refrigerate for at least 30 minutes before serving. Serve with tortilla chips or as a topping for tacos.

Avocado Lime Dip

Ingredients:

- 2 ripe avocados
- 1/4 cup Greek yogurt
- 2 tablespoons lime juice
- 1 clove garlic, minced
- Salt and pepper to taste
- Fresh cilantro for garnish (optional)

Instructions:

1. **Mash Avocados:** In a bowl, mash the avocados with a fork until smooth.
2. **Combine Ingredients:** Add Greek yogurt, lime juice, garlic, salt, and pepper. Mix until well combined.
3. **Taste and Adjust:** Adjust seasoning to taste.
4. **Serve:** Transfer to a serving bowl, garnish with cilantro if desired, and serve with tortilla chips or fresh veggies.

Garlic and Herb Cheese Spread

Ingredients:

- 8 oz cream cheese, softened
- 1/2 cup shredded cheese (e.g., cheddar, mozzarella)
- 2 cloves garlic, minced
- 1 tablespoon fresh herbs (e.g., chives, parsley, thyme), chopped
- Salt and pepper to taste

Instructions:

1. **Combine Ingredients:** In a bowl, mix together cream cheese, shredded cheese, garlic, fresh herbs, salt, and pepper.
2. **Mix Until Smooth:** Stir until well combined and creamy.
3. **Chill and Serve:** Refrigerate for at least 30 minutes before serving. Serve with crackers or bread.

Enjoy these flavorful dips at your next gathering or as a delicious snack!

Chocolate Hummus

Ingredients:

- 1 can (15 oz) chickpeas, drained and rinsed
- 1/4 cup unsweetened cocoa powder
- 1/4 cup maple syrup (or honey)
- 2 tablespoons almond milk (or any milk of choice)
- 1 teaspoon vanilla extract
- A pinch of salt

Instructions:

1. **Blend Ingredients:** In a food processor, combine chickpeas, cocoa powder, maple syrup, almond milk, vanilla extract, and salt.
2. **Process Until Smooth:** Blend until the mixture is completely smooth and creamy. Add more almond milk if needed for desired consistency.
3. **Taste and Adjust:** Adjust sweetness if necessary by adding more maple syrup.
4. **Serve:** Transfer to a bowl and serve with apple slices, pretzels, or graham crackers.

Bacon Cheddar Dip

Ingredients:

- 8 oz cream cheese, softened
- 1 cup shredded sharp cheddar cheese
- 1/2 cup cooked bacon, crumbled
- 1/4 cup sour cream
- 1 tablespoon Worcestershire sauce
- 1/2 teaspoon garlic powder
- Salt and pepper to taste

Instructions:

1. **Combine Ingredients:** In a mixing bowl, combine cream cheese, cheddar cheese, crumbled bacon, sour cream, Worcestershire sauce, garlic powder, salt, and pepper.
2. **Mix Until Smooth:** Stir until well combined and creamy.
3. **Chill and Serve:** Refrigerate for at least 30 minutes before serving. Serve with crackers or vegetables.

Roasted Beet Dip

Ingredients:

- 2 medium beets, roasted and peeled
- 1/2 cup Greek yogurt
- 1 tablespoon lemon juice
- 1 clove garlic, minced
- Salt and pepper to taste
- Fresh dill for garnish (optional)

Instructions:

1. **Blend Ingredients:** In a food processor, combine roasted beets, Greek yogurt, lemon juice, garlic, salt, and pepper.
2. **Process Until Smooth:** Blend until smooth and creamy.
3. **Taste and Adjust:** Adjust seasoning to taste.
4. **Serve:** Transfer to a bowl, garnish with fresh dill if desired, and serve with pita chips or vegetable sticks.

Almond Butter Dip

Ingredients:

- 1/2 cup almond butter
- 1/4 cup Greek yogurt
- 2 tablespoons honey or maple syrup
- 1 tablespoon almond milk (or any milk of choice)
- 1 teaspoon vanilla extract
- A pinch of salt

Instructions:

1. **Combine Ingredients:** In a bowl, mix together almond butter, Greek yogurt, honey, almond milk, vanilla extract, and salt.
2. **Stir Until Smooth:** Whisk until well combined and creamy.
3. **Taste and Adjust:** Adjust sweetness if necessary by adding more honey or maple syrup.
4. **Serve:** Serve with apple slices, pretzels, or graham crackers.

Mustard Herb Dip

Ingredients:

- 1/2 cup Greek yogurt
- 1/4 cup Dijon mustard
- 1 tablespoon honey
- 1 tablespoon apple cider vinegar
- 1 tablespoon fresh herbs (e.g., dill, parsley, chives), chopped
- Salt and pepper to taste

Instructions:

1. **Combine Ingredients:** In a bowl, mix together Greek yogurt, Dijon mustard, honey, apple cider vinegar, fresh herbs, salt, and pepper.
2. **Stir Until Smooth:** Whisk until well combined.
3. **Taste and Adjust:** Adjust seasoning to taste.
4. **Serve:** Serve with fresh vegetables, crackers, or as a sandwich spread.

Honey Walnut Cheese Spread

Ingredients:

- 8 oz cream cheese, softened
- 1/2 cup crumbled blue cheese (or goat cheese)
- 1/4 cup walnuts, chopped
- 2 tablespoons honey
- Salt and pepper to taste

Instructions:

1. **Combine Ingredients:** In a mixing bowl, combine cream cheese, blue cheese, walnuts, honey, salt, and pepper.
2. **Mix Until Smooth:** Stir until well combined and creamy.
3. **Chill and Serve:** Refrigerate for at least 30 minutes before serving. Serve with crackers or baguette slices.

Eggplant Dip (Melitzanosalata)

Ingredients:

- 2 medium eggplants
- 1/4 cup Greek yogurt
- 2 tablespoons lemon juice
- 1 clove garlic, minced
- 2 tablespoons olive oil
- Salt and pepper to taste
- Fresh parsley for garnish (optional)

Instructions:

1. **Roast Eggplants:** Preheat oven to 400°F (200°C). Prick the eggplants with a fork and place them on a baking sheet. Roast for about 30-40 minutes, until soft. Let cool, then scoop out the flesh.
2. **Blend Ingredients:** In a food processor, combine roasted eggplant, Greek yogurt, lemon juice, garlic, olive oil, salt, and pepper.
3. **Process Until Smooth:** Blend until smooth and creamy.
4. **Serve:** Transfer to a bowl, garnish with fresh parsley if desired, and serve with pita bread or fresh vegetables.

Enjoy these delicious dips at your next gathering or as a tasty snack!

Chipotle Lime Avocado Dip

Ingredients:

- 2 ripe avocados
- 1-2 chipotle peppers in adobo sauce (adjust to taste)
- 2 tablespoons lime juice
- 1 clove garlic, minced
- 1/4 teaspoon cumin
- Salt to taste
- Fresh cilantro for garnish (optional)

Instructions:

1. **Prepare Avocados:** Cut the avocados in half, remove the pit, and scoop the flesh into a mixing bowl.
2. **Blend Ingredients:** Add chipotle peppers, lime juice, garlic, cumin, and salt to the bowl.
3. **Mash and Mix:** Use a fork or a potato masher to mash and mix until creamy and well combined.
4. **Taste and Adjust:** Adjust the seasoning if needed.
5. **Serve:** Transfer to a serving bowl and garnish with fresh cilantro. Serve with tortilla chips or fresh vegetables.

Coconut Yogurt Dip

Ingredients:

- 1 cup plain coconut yogurt
- 2 tablespoons honey or maple syrup (adjust to taste)
- 1 teaspoon vanilla extract
- 1/4 teaspoon cinnamon (optional)
- Fresh fruit for dipping (e.g., strawberries, apple slices)

Instructions:

1. **Combine Ingredients:** In a bowl, mix together coconut yogurt, honey or maple syrup, vanilla extract, and cinnamon (if using).
2. **Stir Until Smooth:** Whisk until the mixture is well combined and creamy.
3. **Taste and Adjust:** Adjust sweetness as desired.
4. **Serve:** Serve with fresh fruit for dipping or as a topping for desserts.

Apple Cider Vinegar Dressing Dip

Ingredients:

- 1/4 cup apple cider vinegar
- 1/2 cup olive oil
- 1 tablespoon Dijon mustard
- 1 tablespoon honey or maple syrup
- 1 clove garlic, minced
- Salt and pepper to taste
- Fresh herbs (e.g., parsley, thyme) for garnish (optional)

Instructions:

1. **Combine Ingredients:** In a mixing bowl or jar, combine apple cider vinegar, olive oil, Dijon mustard, honey or maple syrup, garlic, salt, and pepper.
2. **Whisk or Shake:** Whisk together or seal the jar and shake until emulsified and well combined.
3. **Taste and Adjust:** Adjust seasoning if necessary.
4. **Serve:** Serve as a dip for fresh vegetables or as a salad dressing. Garnish with fresh herbs if desired.

Enjoy these flavorful dips at your next gathering or as delicious snacks!